WONDERS
OF THE
WORLD

WONDERS OF THE WORLD

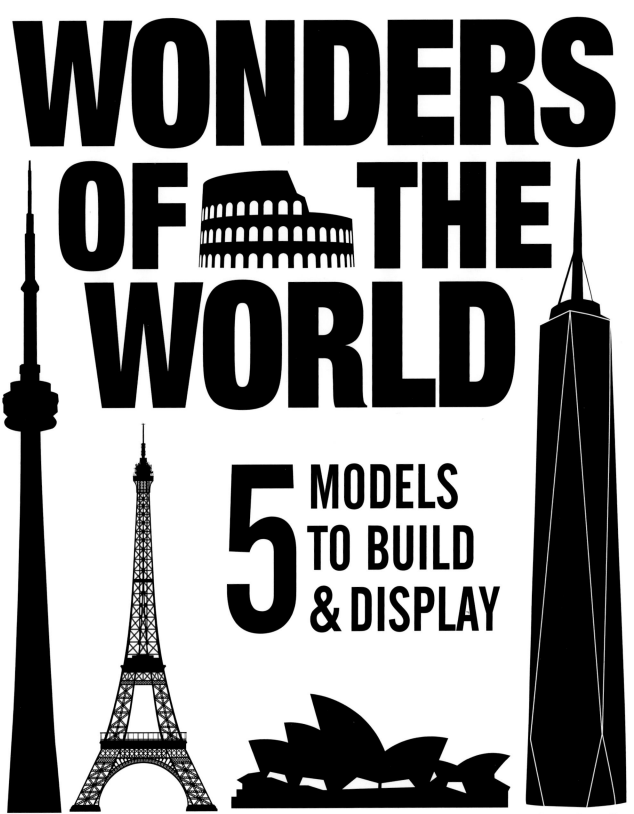

5 MODELS TO BUILD & DISPLAY

Keith Finch

CHARTWELL BOOKS

Quarto is the authority on a wide range of topics.

Quarto educates, entertains and enriches the lives of our readers—enthusiasts and lovers of hands-on living.

www.quartoknows.com

Published in 2016 by arrangement with BlueRed Press Ltd.
The Wonders of the World by Keith Finch

First published in the United States of America in 2016 by
Chartwell Books,
an imprint of Book Sales
a division of Quarto Publishing Group USA Inc.
142 West 36th Street, 4th Floor
New York, New York 10018

quartoknows.com

10 9 8 7 6 5 4 3 2 1

ISBN: 978-0-7858-3396-3

Printed in China

Paper engineering, text, design and layout © 2016 BlueRed Press Ltd
Paper engineering Keith Finch
Design and illustration Insight Design Concepts Ltd

Contents

6   Introduction

8   The Colosseum

16   Eiffel Tower

24   Sydney Opera House

32   CN Tower

40   One World Trade Center

49   Colosseum press-out pieces

61   Eiffel Tower press-out pieces

73   Sydney Opera House press-out pieces

85   CN Tower press-out pieces

97   One World Trade Center press-out pieces

Introduction

Since ancient times, humankind has striven to produce works of architecture to dazzle and amaze, their size and artistry symbolizing the earthly power and wealth of their builders. From vast pyramids and harbor-straddling colossi to magnificent cathedrals and towers that scrape the sky, human history has been written in stone and concrete and glass and steel.

Over the millennia various lists have been compiled, confidently cataloging the most wondrous of the world's preeminent works of architecture. All have failed. The ancient guidebook writers who promoted the Seven Wonders of the World to early sightseers had no way to compare the Egyptian pyramids with the great building works of Asia or South America. Later attempts such as the New Seven Wonders of the World seem arbitrary and have shocking omissions: why does Angkor Wat not appear? Or the Acropolis in Athens? Or the Alhambra? And that's just the "A's." In truth, any attempt to create a concrete list of the world's wonders will always be doomed. The list itself might be manipulated (some reports claim that 14 million Jordanians voted for Petra to be included on the new list of seven wonders, despite the country having a total population of only 7 million). Some buildings will be tragically overlooked; new and even more splendid constructions, or freshly discovered archeological sites, might make the list look out-of-date as soon as it is complete.

Lists are flawed, and – in truth – don't really matter very much. **Wonders of the World**, doesn't pretend to offer a cast-iron selection of the world's greatest wonders. Some of the five amazing buildings selected here do appear on "definitive" lists of the world's great monuments – the Colosseum is both an acknowledged wonder of the world and a UNESCO World Heritage site – others appear on none: while it is undoubtedly an architectural and engineering marvel, as well as a testament to the courage and resilience of the United States, One World Trade Center has yet to be honored with a place on any official list of wonders. What this book does offer is a unique celebration of five of the world's greatest works of architecture as well as hours of creative play.

There are any number of thick tomes covering the world's great works of architecture in dry detail, but **Wonders of the World** offers something a little different – the chance to get up close to the buildings by constructing your own models. The five buildings included are among the planet's best-known and most striking: The Eiffel Tower, Canada's CN Tower, One World Trade Center, Sydney Opera House, and the Colosseum. Each is accompanied by facts and figures that give some background information to bring your very own miniature wonder alive. Chosen for their fame, and beauty, and the sheer joy that piecing them together will bring, this selection of buildings is as valid as any ancient catalog of the world's wonders and a lot more fun!

The Colosseum

QUICK FACTS

Location:	Rome, Italy
Built by:	Emperors Vespasian, Titus, and Domitian
Designed:	72 CE
Completed:	80 CE
Material:	Travertine stone, concrete, and sand
Height:	157 feet (48 m)
Length:	615 feet (189 m)
Width:	519 feet (156 m)
Area:	Six acres (24,000 sq m)

One of the Seven New Wonders of the World and a UNESCO World Heritage Site

Originally known as the Amphitheatrum Flavium (Flavian Amphitheater), the iconic Colosseum is the largest of its kind ever built and an enduring monument to the power, artistry, and engineering skills of Ancient Rome. Once a stage for fierce gladiatorial combat and executions, the building's grace and grandeur belie a history of bloodshed and violence.

Construction began in 72 CE, by command of the Emperor Vespasian. The space that the massive new amphitheater was to fill had been previously appropriated from the city by the hated Nero after the great fire of Rome in 64 CE. Nero had subsequently built a palace and pleasure

garden for himself on the site, and Vespasian's decision to tear it down and replace it with a venue for public entertainment signaled his desire to distance himself from his predecessor. Financed by booty taken from Jerusalem following the Great Jewish Revolt of 70 CE, and erected by tens of thousands of Jewish slaves working alongside paid Roman artisans, the finished amphitheater occupied six acres with support buildings and a gladiator school close by. The exterior walls are of travertine stone and were built without using mortar, the ground level featuring eighty entrances for spectators. Rising in three rows of arched arcades, the walls enclose an arena that measured 287 feet (87 m) by 180 feet (55 m) surrounded by tiered seating reserved for citizens of different classes (with the poorest in the higher seats farthest from the action). At either end were special boxes – one for the emperor and one for the Vestal Virgins.

Vespasian died in 79 CE and work was finished under his son, Titus, in 80 CE. Titus's brother, Domitian, later constructed the hypogeum: a two-level subterranean warren of tunnels, cages, and chambers that housed gladiators, slaves, and animals. Estimates of the amphiteater's capacity range from 50,000 to 80,000 spectators, but no one disputes its instant popularity. At the inaugural games alone it is reported that over 9,000 wild beasts were slaughtered for the entertainment of the crowds. Seated beneath a retractable awning that provided shade, Roman spectators would have bayed and cursed at the sight of human warriors (including female gladiators) fighting each other, as well as beasts from across the empire, including crocodiles, tigers, elephants, and rhinoceros. Staging would have been elaborate with painters and stage technicians providing a range of natural-looking scenes, while it is thought that the arena could be flooded so that mock sea-battles could be held. Interval entertainments included the executions of criminals. Despite bloodshed on such a vast scale, however, there is no documented evidence that the Colosseum was ever used for the mass execution of Christians. Although some martyrs must have met their

Left: The most impressive building of Rome's early imperial era, today the half-ruined Colosseum is a stunning reminder of Roman ingenuity and artistry.

Right: The facade of the Colosseum is ringed with three levels of arches. Marble and other building materials were pillaged from the building and used in the construction of later landmarks such as St. Peter's Basilica.

end here, most are thought to have died at amphitheaters such as the Circus Maximus outside the center of the city.

Over the following centuries the Colosseum witnessed the deaths of countless humans and animals, though with the rise of Christianity spectacles more and more often involved animal hunts. The last such entertainment is thought to have been staged in the early sixth century CE. In subsequent years, the Colosseum was used for other purposes, variously housing workshops, a religious order, and a Christian shrine, and was quarried extensively for stone to build other monuments around the city. Today, it is Rome's greatest tourist attraction and also houses a museum to Eros. Fittingly, this site of bloodshed has also become a symbol for anti-capital punishment campaigners. Now, whenever a prisoner's death penalty is commuted anywhere in the world, or when a state abolishes the death penalty, the Colosseum's walls are lit with gold light at night.

Right: An aerial view showing the interior of the Colosseum. The surface of the arena has gone, leaving exposed the cells below, which once would have held wild animals, convicted criminals, and gladiators waiting their turn to fight before Rome's baying crowds.

Below: The Colosseum lit at night with golden light, signaling that somewhere in the world a prisoner has been spared the death penalty.

⌂This symbol indicates that there are folds that should be made on the piece/s before carrying out the instructions.

1. ⌂

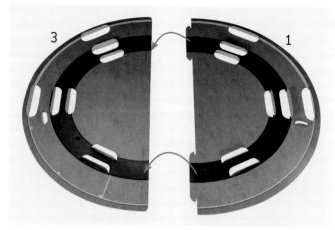

⌂Insert the A tabs on piece 3 into the A slots on piece 1.

2. ⌂

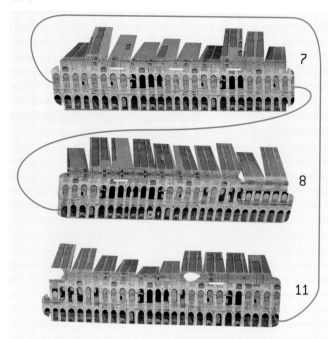

⌂Insert tab A on piece 7 into slot A on piece 8.
Insert tab B on piece 7 into slot B on piece 11.

3.

Insert tab C on piece 11 into slot C on piece 8.

4.

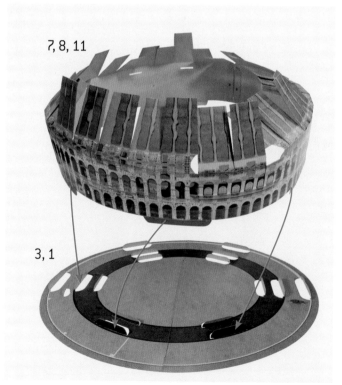

Place the combined pieces 7, 8, and 11 onto the base with the following tabs and slots matched up: D, E, F, G, H, and I.

5. ⌃

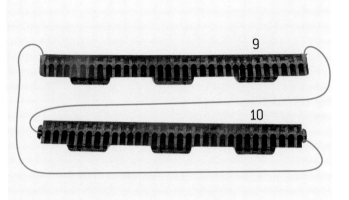

Slot tab A on piece 9 into slot A on piece 10.
Slot tab B on piece 9 into slot B on piece 10.

6. ⌃

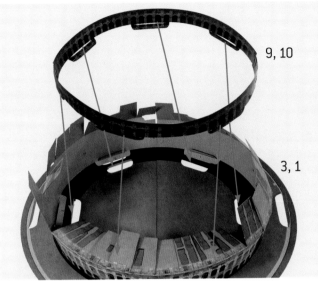

Make sure that the flaps on pieces 9 and 10 are facing outward, as shown in the illustration.
Place the combined pieces 9 and 10 onto the base with the following tabs and slots matched up: P, Q, R, S, T, and U.
Make sure that you keep the flaps on top of the outer ring (pieces 7, 8, and 11) inside the inner ring (pieces 9 and 10) as you make the connections.

7. ⌃

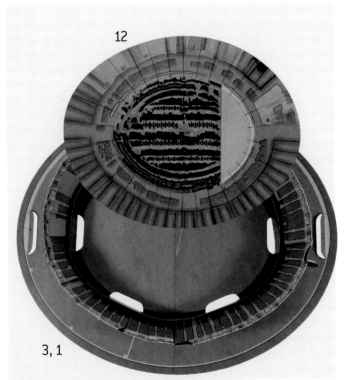

⌃ Place piece 12 into the model, as shown in the illustration. Make sure that the end of piece 12 with sand is on the same side of the model as tab L on the base.

8. ⌃

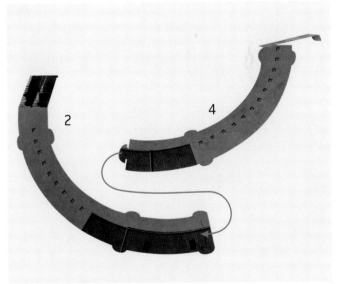

Insert tab A on piece 4 into slot A on piece 2.

9.

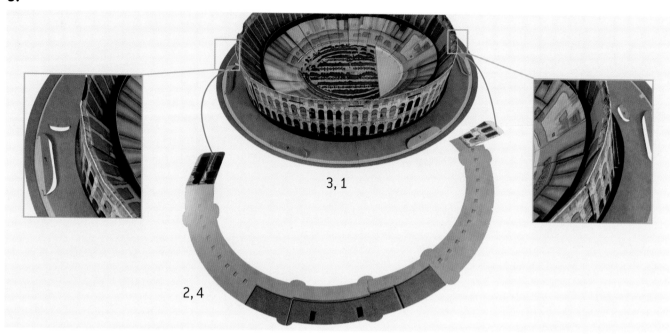

3, 1

2, 4

Connect pieces 2 and 4 to the model as shown in the illustration.
Slot J on piece 2 connects with tab J on piece 3.
Slot K on piece 4 connects with tab K on piece 1.

10.

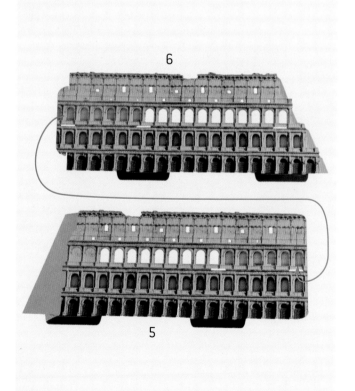

6

5

Connect piece 5 to piece 6, as shown in the illustration.

11.

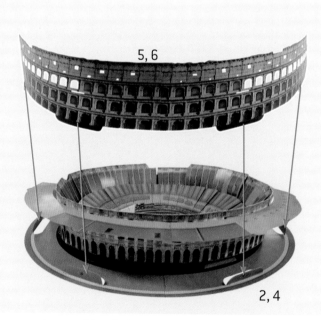

5, 6

2, 4

Connect the combined pieces 5 and 6 to the model with the following tabs and slots matched: L, M, N, and O. Push the lugs on the inner section through the slots on pieces 5 and 6 as you go around.

12.

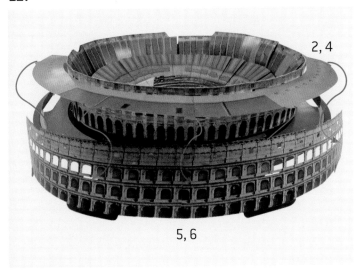

Push the lugs on the inner wall through the slots on pieces 5 and 6.

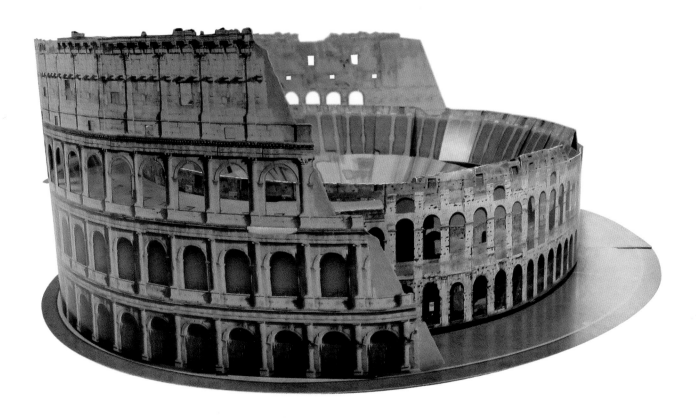

Eiffel Tower

QUICK FACTS

Location: Paris, France
Architects: Maurice Koechlin, Émile Nouguier,
                  Stephen Sauvestre
Designed: 1884
Completed: 1889
Material: Wrought iron
Height: 1,063 feet (324 m) – including antennas
Weight: 10,100 tons

Part of the Paris, Banks of the Seine UNESCO World
Heritage Site

The Eiffel Tower defines the skyline of Paris so powerfully that it is almost impossible to imagine the city without its 1,063-foot (324-m) wrought-iron tower. Attracting more than 250 million visitors since it opened for the city's Universal Exhibition of 1889, the tower is now such an integral part of Paris that it is easy to forget that the city has not always been so proud of its most prominent feature. Indeed, when the design was first unveiled many Parisian artists and architects responded with a petition to prevent its construction. The writer Guy de Maupassant is famously said to have been so appalled by it that he ate lunch at the tower's restaurant every

day after it was erected saying "it is the one place in Paris from which the tower is not visible." Such objections, however, proved to be short-lived and for more than a century the beautiful, latticed spike has towered above the city, providing Paris with a visually stunning centerpiece.

The concept of a vast tower that would form the focal point of the city's 1889 World's Fair exhibition came in 1884, and was not — as is widely thought — the idea of Gustave Eiffel, but that of Maurice Koechlin, an engineer who worked at Eiffel's company. Koechlin's first sketch showed "a great pylon, consisting of four lattice girders standing apart at the base and coming together at the top, joined together by metal trusses at regular intervals" and was developed with the help of Émile Nouguier. Eiffel himself was not entirely convinced by the plan but warmed to the design after Stephen Sauvestre, the company's chief architect, had embellished the drawings. Eiffel purchased the patent and, on January 8, 1887, signed a contract to build the tower.

Construction began just twenty days later, beginning with the laying of six-and-a-half-foot (2-m) foundations for each of the tower's four feet into which "shoes" for the superstructure were fitted with twenty-five-foot (7.6-m) long bolts. With the groundwork completed by June 30, over the following twenty-one months 300 workers fitted 18,038 parts together with incredible precision using 2.5 million rivets. Throughout the process, Eiffel insisted on safety. Only one man died during construction.

Structural work (including a private apartment for Eiffel) was completed on March 30, 1889, although the lifts were not yet operational. On May 6, the Exposition Universelle opened and nine days later the Eiffel Tower — then the tallest building in the world — opened to the public. As the lifts were still not working they had to climb its stairs. It was, however, an instant and massive success. By the time the exhibition ended just under two million visitors had paid the entrance fee (five francs each to ascend all the way to the top, two francs for the first level, and three for the second) to experience the magnificent views the tower offered. When darkness fell, hundreds of gas lamps

Left: Originally intended to stand for just twenty years, the Eiffel Tower (also known as La Dame de Fer or "Iron Lady") remains the focal point of the Parisian cityscape more than a century after its completion.

Right: The tower was finished in 1889 and was the tallest building in the world until the Chrysler Building in New York City opened in 1930.

illuminated the city's new marvel, while beacons beamed the red, white, and blue of the French *Tricolore* into the sky.

By the time the tower's twenty-year permit expired in 1909 even some of the most vociferous of its opponents had been won over by the landmark's elegant beauty, and its usefulness to the city for communications and meteorology meant that demolition was indefinitely postponed. Today, it is the most-visited pay-to-enter attraction in the world and widely regarded as a symbol of Paris and of France.

Right: The Eiffel Tower lit up in the red, white, and blue of the French Tricolore to commemorate the victims of the Paris attacks of November, 2015.

Below right: The graceful iron lattice of the Eiffel Tower pictured from beneath. Engraved into the tower's ironwork are the names of the seventy-two engineers, mathematicians, and scientists who contributed to the construction.

Below: At the foot of the Eiffel Tower lies the Champ de Mars ("Field of Mars"), which was once used as a drill ground for French troops. This view shows the park from the top level of the tower.

⬢ This symbol indicates that there are folds that should be made on the piece/s before carrying out the instructions.

1. ⬢

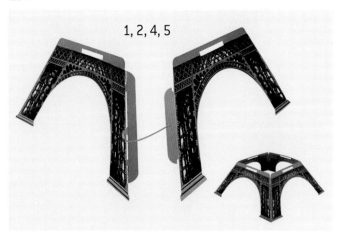

1, 2, 4, 5

Insert tab A on piece 2 into Slot A on piece 1.
Insert tab B on piece 1 into Slot B on piece 4.
Insert tab C on piece 4 into slot C on piece 5.
Insert tab D on piece 5 into slot D on piece 2.

2. ⬢

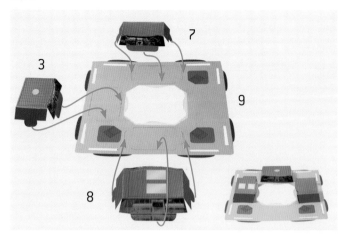

3   7   9   8

Insert tabs A, B, C, and D on piece 3 into the corresponding slots on piece 9.
Insert tabs E, F, G, and H on piece 8 into corresponding slots on piece 9.
Insert tabs I, J, K, and L on piece 7 into corresponding slots on piece 9.

3. ⬢

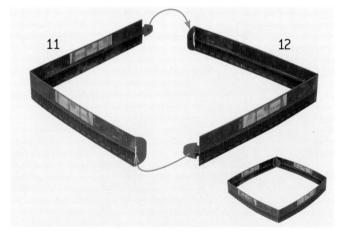

11   12

Insert tab A on piece 11 into slot A on piece 12.
Insert tab B on piece 12 into slot B on piece 11.

4.

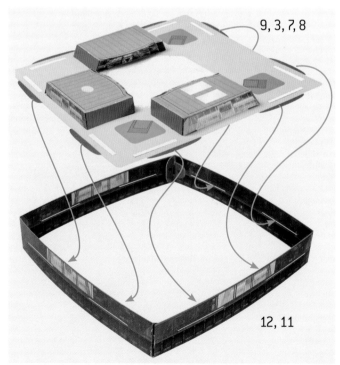

9, 3, 7, 8

12, 11

Connect pieces 11 and 12 to piece 9 by inserting the outer tabs on piece 9 into the slots on pieces 11 and 12. Ensure that the blue dots on pieces 9 and 11 are on the same side of the square.

5.

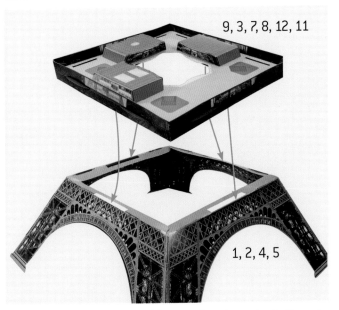

9, 3, 7, 8, 12, 11

1, 2, 4, 5

Place the piece assembled in step 4, using tabs C, E, and K protruding out of the bottom of piece 9; Please note that although there are four slots you only need to use three and that it doesn't matter which tabs go into which of the four slots.

6.

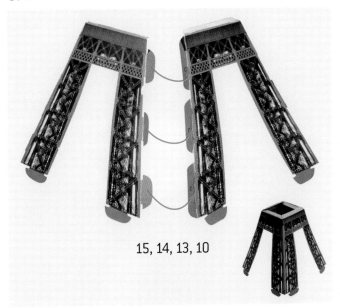

15, 14, 13, 10

Insert the A tabs on piece 15 into the A slots on piece 14.
Insert the B tabs on piece 14 into the B slots on piece 13.
Insert the C tabs on piece 13 into the C slots on piece 10.
Insert the D tabs on piece 10 into the D slots on piece 15.

7.

6

Fold piece 6 back on itself as shown in the illustration.

8.

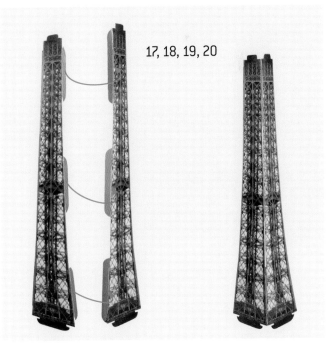

17, 18, 19, 20

Insert the A tabs on piece 18 into the A slots on piece 17.
Insert the B tabs on piece 17 into the B slots on piece 19.
Insert the C tabs on piece 19 into the C slots on piece 20.
Insert the D tabs on piece 20 into the D slots on piece 18.

9. ◈

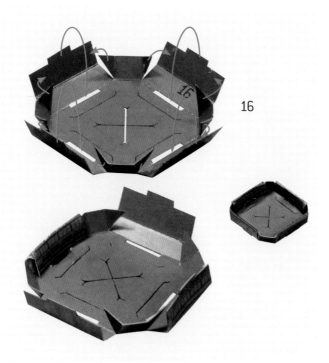

16

Fold piece 16 back on itself as shown in the illustration.

10.

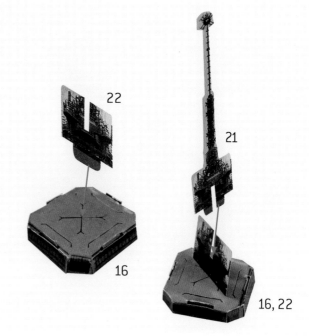

22

21

16

16, 22

Slot piece 22 into piece 16. It doesn't matter which tabs go into which slots.
Slot piece 21 into piece 22 and then into the two remaining slots on piece 16.

11.

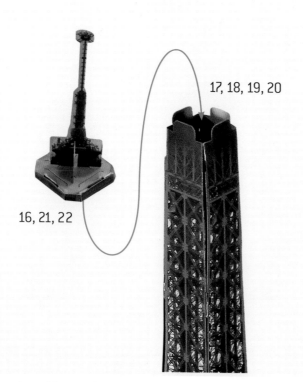

17, 18, 19, 20

16, 21, 22

Slot piece 16 onto the tabs on top of pieces 17, 18, 19, and 20. It doesn't matter which tabs go into which slots.

12.

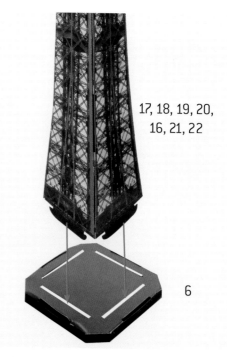

17, 18, 19, 20, 16, 21, 22

6

Push the tabs on the bottom of pieces 17, 18, 19, and 20 into the slots on piece 6. It doesn't matter which tabs go into which slots. Then push the tabs on the bottom of pieces 17, 18, 19, and 20 into the slots on pieces 10, 16, 14, and 15. It doesn't matter which tabs go into which slots.

13.

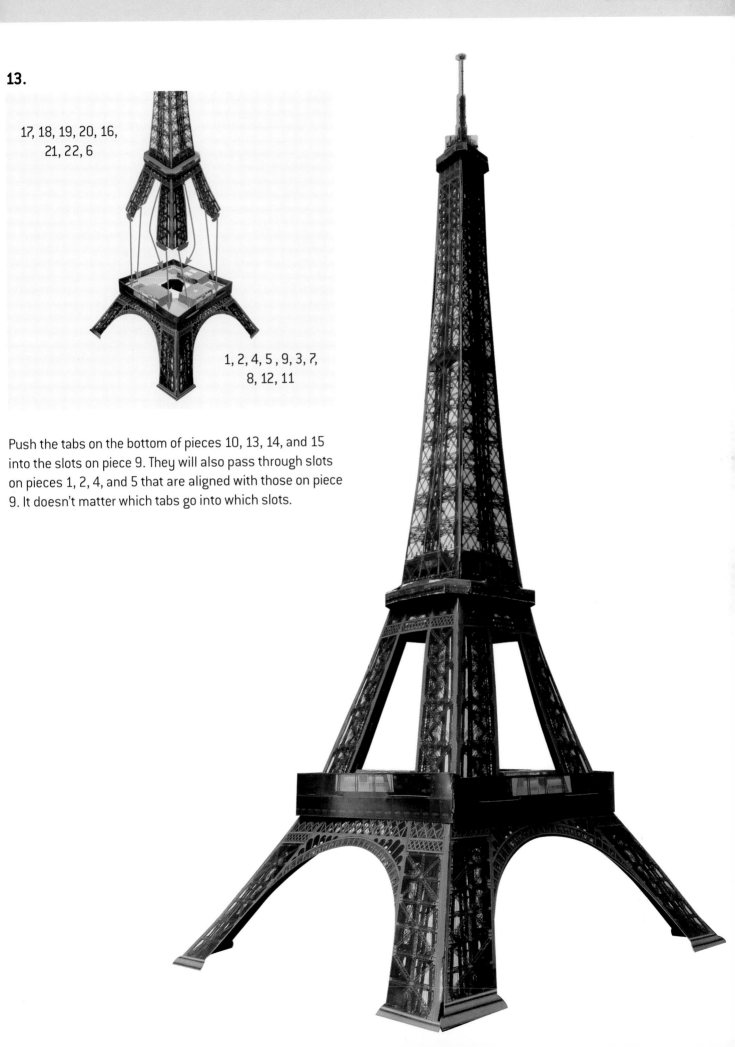

17, 18, 19, 20, 16, 21, 22, 6

1, 2, 4, 5 , 9, 3, 7, 8, 12, 11

Push the tabs on the bottom of pieces 10, 13, 14, and 15 into the slots on piece 9. They will also pass through slots on pieces 1, 2, 4, and 5 that are aligned with those on piece 9. It doesn't matter which tabs go into which slots.

Sydney Opera House

QUICK FACTS

Location:	Sydney, Australia
Architect:	Jørn Utzon
Designed:	1956
Completed:	1973
Material:	Concrete ceiling beams and roof sections, over 1 million roof tiles, steel cable, and glass
Height:	220 feet (67 m)
Length:	613 feet (187 m)
Width:	377 feet (115 m)

A UNESCO World Heritage Site

Rumored to have been salvaged from a pile of discarded ideas when the competition to design Sydney's opera house was organized in 1956, the eventual winner is a testament to the bold vision of its architect. Soaring over the waters of Sydney Harbor, the distinctive interlocking "shells" of its roofline, which have been likened to the sails of a tall ship, are a defining feature of the cityscape and make the opera house one of the most recognized buildings in the world. Graceful, dramatic, and explosively unexpected, the Sydney Opera House is universally accepted as a true masterpiece of modern architecture.

Today, the building is a treasured feature of the city, but its construction was mired in difficulty. Danish architect Jørn Utzon's plan was selected from 233 proposed designs in 1957 but it would take sixteen years to complete the building, during which work was hampered by structural problems, blown budgets, and the architect himself resigning. The problems began in March 1959 when construction of the podium on which the opera house would sit started before Utzon had finished drawing up the final plans. Improper planning meant that supporting columns would later have to be replaced, and construction was also slowed by legal issues and bad weather as well as unexpected engineering problems.

After the podium was finished in 1963, more difficulties arose. Utzon's unique vision meant that equally unique engineering solutions had to be found to realize the

Above: Sydney Opera House occupies a promontory called Bennelong Point which juts into Sydney Harbour. Originally a small, rocky island, the point was once the home of Fort Macquarie and, later, was used as a tram depot.

Left: Designed by Peter Hall (Utzon's successor), Sydney Opera House features 67,000 square feet (6,225 sq m) of glass, which was specially made in France.

flamboyant design. Building the distinctive "shells" was, in short, one of the most complicated architectural engineering projects ever to have been attempted at that time. Finding an economically acceptable way to manufacture and erect the shells took six years, during which twelve different designs were explored before Utzon and his team came up with a solution that meant all the necessary arches could be cast in the same mold. New computer technology helped to analyze the structure and extensive tests on scale models were carried out in a wind tunnel at Southampton University on the other side of the planet.

Both the work and the budget had already overrun by 1966. Faced with mounting criticism from the government and public, Utzon resigned, leaving a committee of new architects to finish the building's glass walls and interiors. In 1957, the cost of the new Sydney Opera House had been estimated at $AUS 7.5 million. Its projected completion date had been January 26, 1963 (Australia Day). By the time the building was finally opened by Queen Elizabeth II more than a decade late on October 20, 1973, its cost had ballooned to over $AUS 100 million. Utzon was not invited to the ceremony.

Nevertheless, he had given Sydney an architectural gem. Clad with off-white tiles that blaze beneath the Australian sun, the Opera House's sculptural roofline is a magnificent focal point against the backdrop of Sydney Harbor. Containing two main auditoria as well as other performance and rehearsal spaces along with cafés, bars, and retail space, the building has become a cultural hub for the city and is celebrated throughout the world for its superlative design. In the words of Frank Gehry, "Utzon made a building well ahead of its time, far ahead of available technology, and he persevered through extraordinarily malicious publicity and negative criticism to build a building that changed the image of an entire country."

Utzon died in Copenhagen in 2008. He had never seen the completed opera house in situ, but had lived to see his worked honored as a UNESCO World Heritage Site.

Right: In recent years, Sydney Opera House has invited artists from around the world to use its white-tiled "sails" as a screen on which to project stunning images.

Below: Designed in the Expressionist Modernist style, the "sails" of the Sydney Opera House are covered with more than a million tiles, made-to-order by the Swedish company, Höganas. Despite the difficulties overcome during its construction, it is today one of the world's most instantly recognizable, and best-loved, buildings.

⬢ This symbol indicates that there are folds that should be made on the piece/s before carrying out the instructions.

1. ⬢

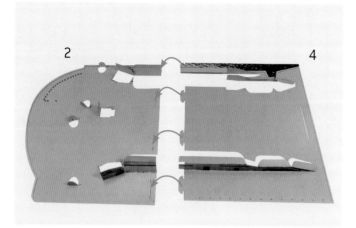

Insert the A tabs on piece 4 into the A slots on piece 2.

2. ⬢

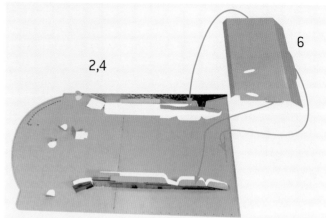

Insert the B tabs on piece 6 into the B tabs on piece 4.

3. ⬢

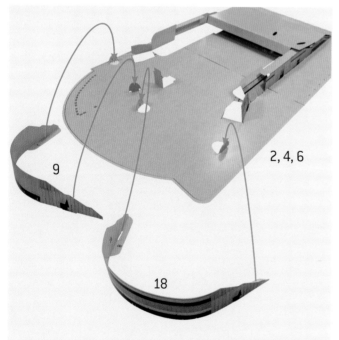

Insert the B tabs on piece 2 into the B slots on piece 18.
Insert the C tabs on piece 9 into the C tabs on piece 4.

4. ⬢

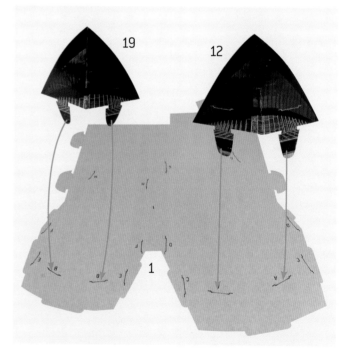

Insert the A tabs on piece 12 into the A slots on piece 1.
Insert the B tabs on piece 19 into the B tabs on piece 1.

5. ⌃

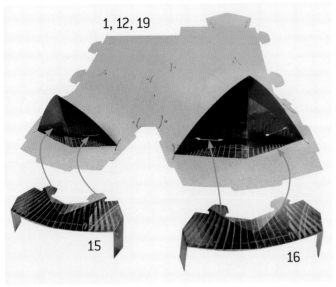

1, 12, 19

15

16

Slot piece 16 into piece 12.
Slot piece 15 into piece 19.

6. ⌃

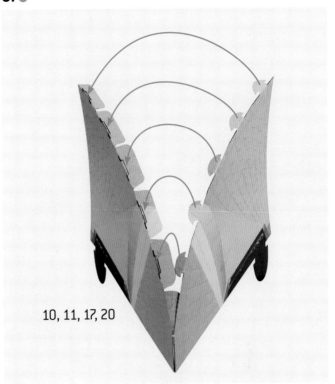

10, 11, 17, 20

Connect the two halves of pieces 10, 11, 17, and 20, as shown in the illustration.

7. ⌃

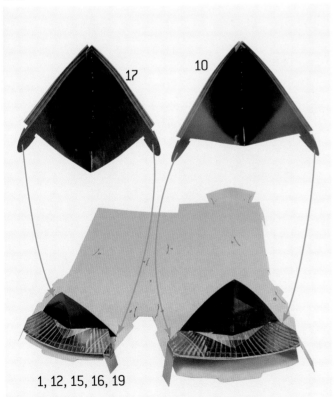

17

10

1, 12, 15, 16, 19

Insert the C slots on piece 10 into the C slots on piece 1.
Insert the E tabs on piece 17 into the E slots on piece 1.

8. ⌃

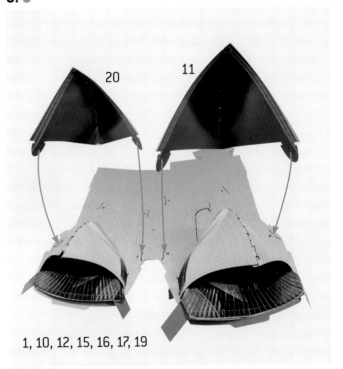

20

11

1, 10, 12, 15, 16, 17, 19

Insert the D tabs on piece 11 into the D slots on piece 1.
Insert the F tabs on piece 20 into the F slots on piece 1.

9. ⌂

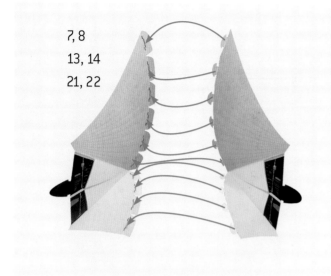

7, 8

13, 14

21, 22

Connect pieces 7 and 8, as shown in the illustration. Repeat with pieces 13 and 14 and then pieces 21 and 22.

10.

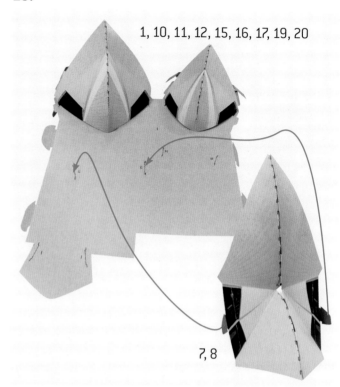

1, 10, 11, 12, 15, 16, 17, 19, 20

7, 8

Insert the G(1 and 2) tabs on pieces 7 and 8 into the corresponding slots on piece 1.

11.

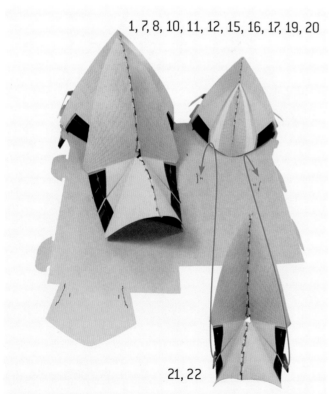

1, 7, 8, 10, 11, 12, 15, 16, 17, 19, 20

21, 22

Insert the H(1 and 2) tabs on pieces 21 and 22 into the corresponding slots on piece 1.

12.

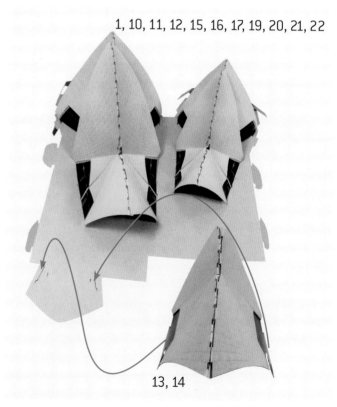

1, 10, 11, 12, 15, 16, 17, 19, 20, 21, 22

13, 14

Insert the I(1 and 2) tabs on pieces 13 and 14 into the corresponding slots on piece 1.

13.

1, 10, 11, 12, 13, 14, 15,
16, 17, 19, 20, 21, 22

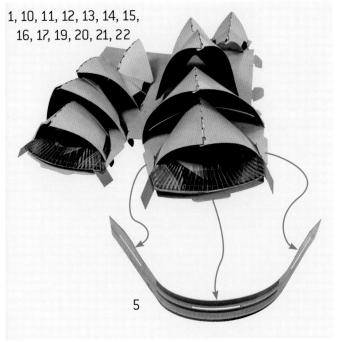

5

Connect piece 5 to piece 1, as shown in the illustration.

14.

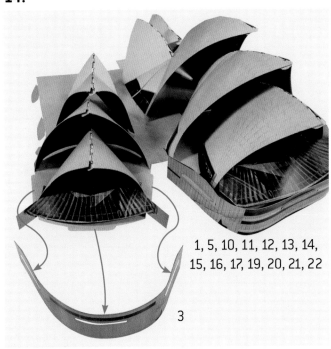

1, 5, 10, 11, 12, 13, 14,
15, 16, 17, 19, 20, 21, 22

3

Connect piece 3 to piece 1, as shown in the illustration.

15.

2, 4, 6, 9, 18, 19

1, 3, 5, 10, 11, 12, 13, 14,
15, 16, 17, 19, 20, 21, 22

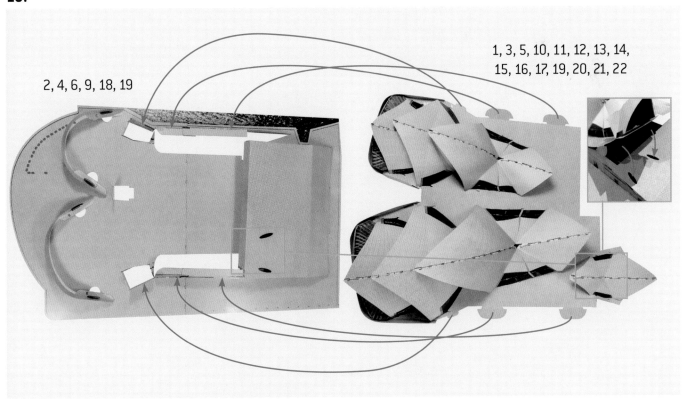

Connect piece 1 to pieces 2 and 4, as shown in the
illustration/s.

CN Tower

QUICK FACTS

Location: Toronto, Canada

Built by: Canadian National Railways with various
                 engineering and architectural companies.

Designed: 1968–72

Completed: 1976

Material: Concrete, wood, and steel

Height: 1,815.4 feet (553.33 m)

One of the Seven Wonders of the Modern World

Below: At 1,815.4 feet (553.33 m), the CN Tower dominates the Toronto skyline.

The world's tallest structure for thirty-four years (from its completion in 1976 to 2010), Toronto's CN Tower remains the highest free-standing building in the western hemisphere. Dominating the city's skyline, it is a much-loved Canadian treasure and a symbol of both the country's economic confidence and engineering prowess.

During the 1960s, Canada experienced an economic boom. At the beginning of the decade the city's skyline was relatively ground-hugging, but, fueled by a new industrial strength, a new forest of skyscrapers quickly rose, rendering Toronto's older telecommunications system largely redundant. The dish antennae of the

point-to-point microwave system, fixed to older buildings, were simply crowded out by the soaring new buildings. In response, Canadian National Railway proposed a tower that would, at a stroke, solve the city's communication problems while simultaneously demonstrating the strength of Canadian industry (the Canadian National Railway in particular).

Initially designed as a shorter, tripod, building, the plans for the new CN Tower evolved into something far more ambitious while the team of architects worked. As realization dawned that the building could become the tallest in the world without being prohibitively more expensive, the design progressed into the tower that now reaches high above Toronto's skyline: a simple, hexagonal, concrete core with three curved support arms, rising to a multi-level enclosed SkyPod (originally called the Space Deck), containing a revolving restaurant and observation deck. Above the SkyPod, the tower rises further, finishing with an elegant spike that hosts an advanced communications array.

Construction began on February 5, 1973. Beginning with the removal of a vast amount of earth and shale for the tower's foundation, the main shaft was constructed by means of an innovative "slipform" device. Over the following months a team of more than 1,500 workers poured concrete, day and night, into a mold that gradually raised itself on hydraulic jacks as the concrete dried, decreasing in size as it rose. A year and a half later, in August 1974, work commenced on the SkyPod level. Vast steel and wooden brackets were lifted into position around the top of the concrete shaft, forming a "crown" frame that supported the structure. The final piece of the CN Tower — its soaring antenna — was lifted into place in thirty-six pieces by a Sikorsky S64 Skycrane helicopter nicknamed "Olga", a process that was not without incident. On its first trip to remove the first part of the crane that was originally intended to place the antenna in position, the crane twisted, making release from the tower impossible. The crane's operator and Olga were trapped high above the city with sufficient fuel for only fifty minutes of flight. Thankfully, the tower's heroic steel workers managed to

burn off the bolts holding the crane in place with fourteen minutes to spare.

On April 2, 1975, the tower was "topped out" when the final piece of the antenna was lowered into place after just twenty-six months of construction. At 1,815.4 feet (553.33 m) it became the tallest building in the world. After work on the SkyPod was completed, the tower officially opened to the public on June 26, 1976, and took its long-standing place in the Guinness Book of Records. Truly, a superb example of Canadian know-how, just as its designers intended, the tower was elected one of the Seven Wonders of the Modern World by the American Society of Civil Engineers in 1995.

Left: CN Tower is visited by more than 1.5 million tourists every year. Attractions at the top include the LookOut observation with its magnificent views, three restaurants, and an outdoor terrace that offers the EdgeWalk – the world's highest promenade on a building. It is possible to see more than 100 miles from the observation deck, while the tower's fine-dining restaurant boasts the world's highest wine cellar!

Right: From dusk each evening, CN Tower is lit up by LED lights with a brief light display taking place on the hour. Celebrating the Canadian flag, its usual livery is red and white but around the year the colors change to commemorate special events or memorial days.

Below: Visitors arriving at the CN Tower can shop at the gift store before rocketing to the LookOut level 1,136 feet (346 m) above the city in one of the tower's six glass elevators. From earth to sky, the trip takes a mere fifty-eight seconds.

⬆ This symbol indicates that there are folds that should be made on the piece/s before carrying out the instructions.

1. ⬆

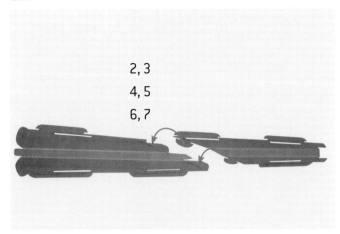

2, 3
4, 5
6, 7

Insert the A tabs on piece 3 into the A slots on piece 2.
Insert the B tabs on piece 5 into the B slots on piece 4.
Insert the C tabs on piece 7 into the C slots on piece 6.

2. ⬆

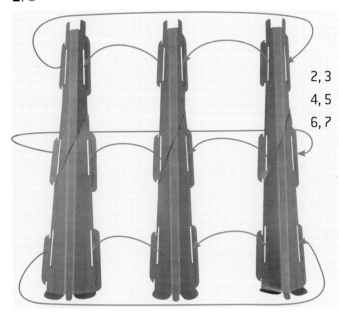

2, 3
4, 5
6, 7

Insert the D tabs on pieces 2 and 3 into the D slots on pieces 4 and 5.
Insert the E tabs on pieces 4 and 5 into the E slots on pieces 6 and 7.
Insert the F tabs on pieces 6 and 7 into the F slots on pieces 2 and 3.

3. ⬆

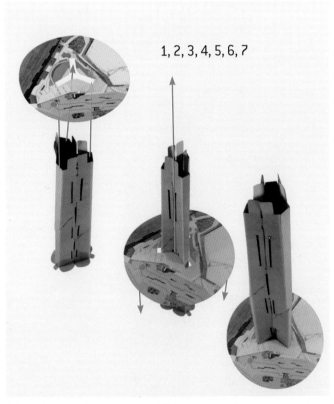

1, 2, 3, 4, 5, 6, 7

Slide piece 1 down the model from top to bottom, as shown in the illustration. This causes the tower to lock into shape.

4. ⬆

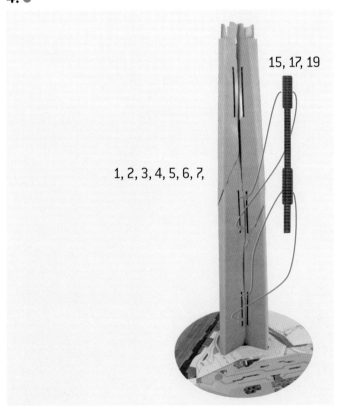

15, 17, 19

1, 2, 3, 4, 5, 6, 7,

Insert pieces 15, 17 and 19 into the model, as shown in the illustration.

5.

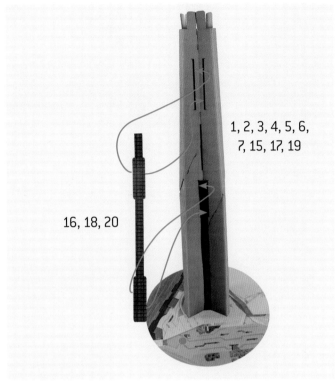

1, 2, 3, 4, 5, 6, 7, 15, 17, 19

16, 18, 20

Insert pieces 16, 18, and 20 into the model, as shown in the illustration.

6.

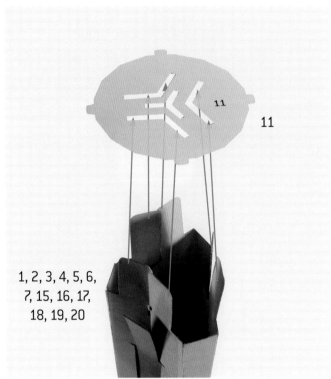

11

1, 2, 3, 4, 5, 6, 7, 15, 16, 17, 18, 19, 20

Place piece 11 on the model, as shown in the illustration.

7.

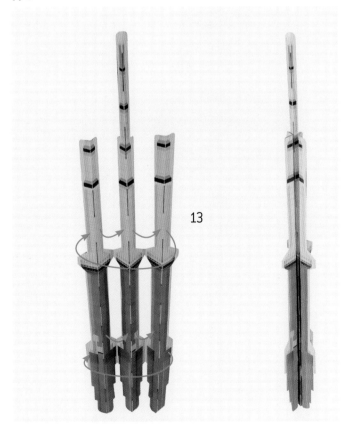

13

Fold piece 13 back on itself, as shown in the illustration.

8.

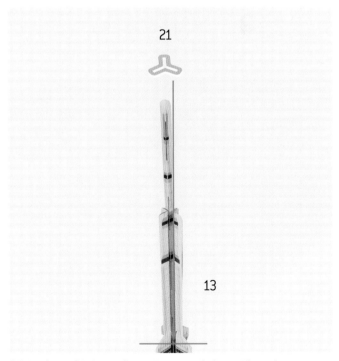

21

13

Slide piece 21 down from the top of piece 13 as far as shown in the diagram, locking the piece together.

9.

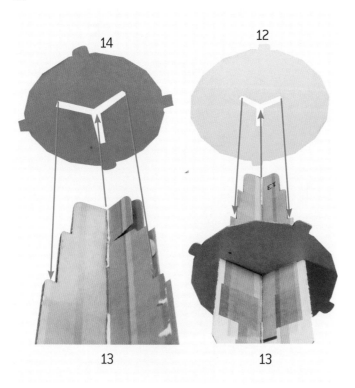

Slot pieces 14 and 12 onto piece 13, as shown in the illustration.

10.

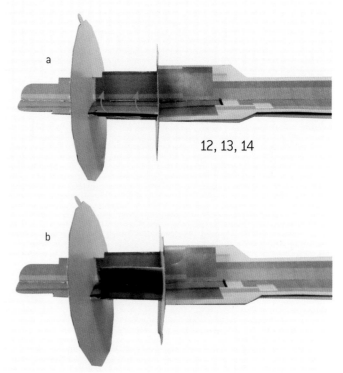

Fold out the flap with the blue dot on it on piece 13, as shown in the illustration.

11. ◈

Wrap piece 9 around piece 12, as shown in the illustration. Make sure that the larger tabs on piece 9 are at the top (sitting under piece 14).

12.

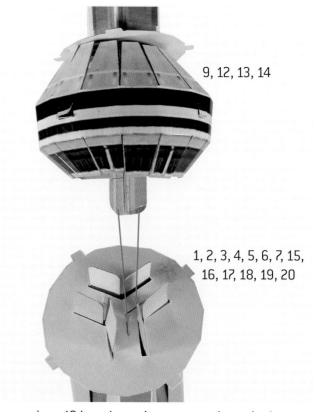

Insert piece 13 into the main tower, as shown in the illustration.

13.

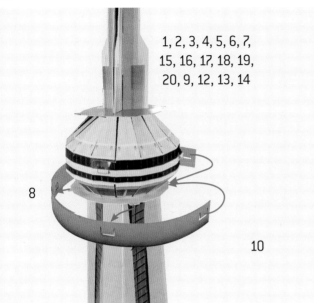

1, 2, 3, 4, 5, 6, 7,
15, 16, 17, 18, 19,
20, 9, 12, 13, 14

8

10

Wrap piece 10 around piece 11, as shown in the illustration.
Make sure that the shadowed edge is at the bottom.

14.

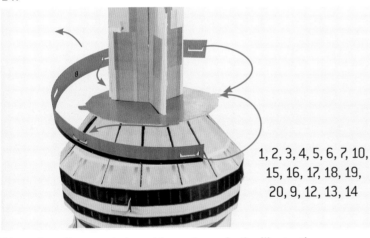

1, 2, 3, 4, 5, 6, 7, 10,
15, 16, 17, 18, 19,
20, 9, 12, 13, 14

Wrap piece 8 around piece 14, as shown in the illustration.

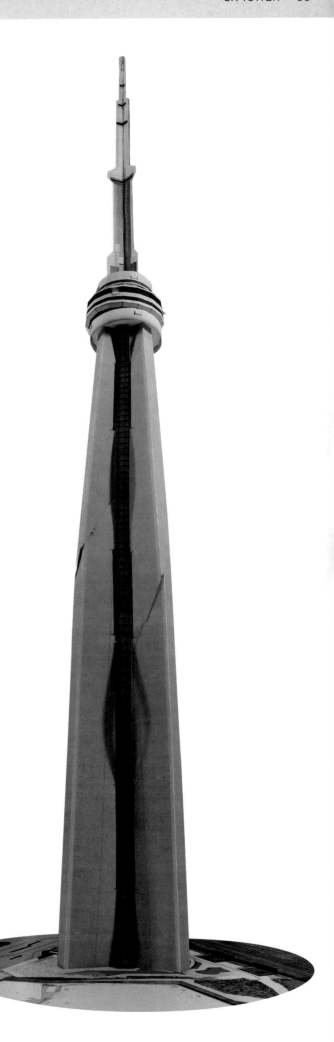

One World Trade Center

QUICK FACTS

Location:	New York City, United States of America
Architects:	David Childs, Skidmore, Owings & Merrill
Designed:	2005
Completed:	2014
Material:	Steel frame, concrete, and glass
Height:	1,776 feet (541 m)
Floors:	104 (94 actual stories)
Area:	approx, 2,600,000 square feet (240,000 sq m)

Standing 1,776 feet tall, the height commemorating the United States Declaration of Independence which was ratified and published in 1776, One World Trade Center stands as a symbol of American defiance on the site of its predecessors – the twin towers that were destroyed in the terrorist attacks of September 11, 2001. Popularly dubbed "Freedom Tower," the skyscraper, with its shining facade and bold form, is the tallest building in the Western hemisphere and has become a New York City landmark since it opened in November, 2014.

Following the tragic attack of 9/11, discussions about what would replace the iconic twin towers began almost before the dust had settled. It was widely agreed that quickly building a new tower would signal the United States' refusal to be cowed by the terrorist atrocity. After several others were rejected, the final design – by David Childs of Skidmore, Owings & Merrill – was presented to the public on June 28, 2005. Described by the architects as a "monolithic glass structure reflecting the sky and topped by a sculpted antenna," the proposed building would echo the simple form of the previous towers while fitting harmoniously into the New York City skyline.

By the time that the plan was unveiled, the cornerstone of the building's foundation had already been laid, during a ceremony in 2004. Subsequent disagreements over design delayed construction work, but on December 18, 2006, a ceremony was held during which members of the public were asked to add their signatures to the first steel beam that would be fitted into the concrete foundation. Construction proceeded smoothly over the following years, aided by a specially designed safety system that protected workers from falling from the swiftly rising tower. By December 2010, it had reached more than 600 feet (180 m) with fifty-two floors completed; by the tenth anniversary of the 9/11 attack it had risen to eighty-two floors. In April 2012, One World Trade Center officially became the tallest building in New York City when it surpassed the 1,250-foot (380-m) roof height of the Empire State Building. The steel structure was completed in August that year, bringing the building's roof height to an imposing 1,368 feet (417 m). When the final piece of the antenna was fitted on May 10, 2013, the building stood at its finished height of 1,776 feet (541 m) and became the sixth tallest in the world. After decorations and interior fittings were finished the skyscraper welcomed its first tenant (the magazine publisher Condé Nast) on November 3, 2014.

Left: At the base of One World Trade Center lies the National September 11 Memorial and Museum, featuring a peaceful landscaped garden. Two square pools were built in the footprints of the twin towers destroyed in the terrorist attack.

Right: Bearing the same name as the original North Tower of the World Trade Center complex, One World Trade Center is the tallest tower in the Western hemisphere and a shining symbol of freedom and resilience.

The finished tower rises from a glass-clad concrete base. At Floor 20, the design departs from the square base, forming eight isosceles triangles (a shape known as an elongated square antiprism). Close to the center, the shape forms an octagon and at the top of the structure a square rotated forty-five degrees from the base square. The 104-story tower boasts almost three million square feet of office space with three observation floors (100, 101, 102). More than 45,000 tons of structural steel and 200,000 square yards of concrete were used in its construction and the building exceeds both the city's safety parameters and its environmental requirements. Fittingly, One World Trade Center contains a steel beam at the top of its structure on which President Barack Obama wrote the words, "We remember, we rebuild, we come back stronger."

Right: An aerial view of New York City's Lower Manhattan area. At 1,776 feet (541 m) the One World Trade Center dwarfs its neighbors.

Below: The Manhattan skyline at dusk, with One World Trade Center at the center. The elegant shape of the tower epitomizes an innovative design which exceeds safety and environmental guidelines. Throughout the day, the faceted, glass-clad exterior reflects the changing skies, producing a kaleidoscopic effect.

◈ This symbol indicates that there are folds that should be made on the piece/s before carrying out the instructions.

1. ◈

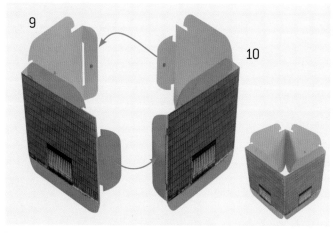

Insert tab A on piece 9 into slot A on piece 10.
Insert tab B on piece 10 into slot B on piece 9.

2. ◈

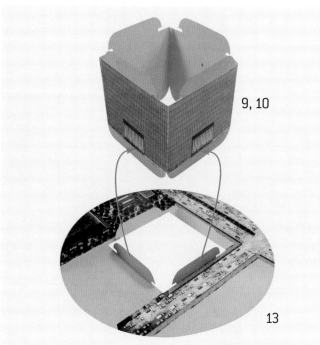

Slot the tabs on piece 13 into the slots at the bottom of pieces 9 and 10. It doesn't matter which tabs go into which slots.

3. ◈

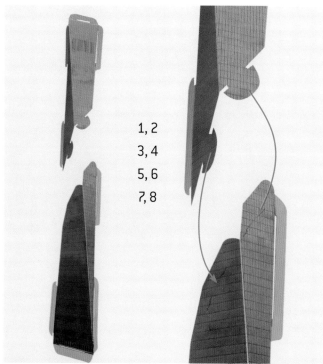

Insert tabs A and B on piece 1 into slots A and B on piece 2.
Insert tabs C and D on piece 3 into slots C and D on piece 4.
Insert tabs E and F on piece 5 into slots E and F on piece 6.
Insert tabs G and H on piece 7 into slots G and H on piece 8.

4.

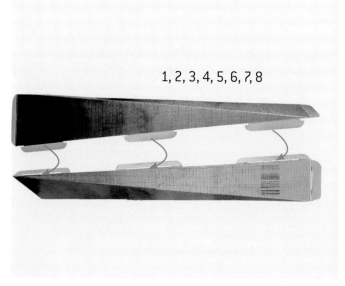

Insert the I tabs on pieces 7 and 8 into the I slots on pieces 1 and 2.
Insert the J tabs on pieces 3 and 4 into the J slots on pieces 5 and 6.
Insert the K tabs on pieces 5 and 6 into the K slots on pieces 7 and 8.
Insert the L tabs on pieces 1 and 2 into the L slots on pieces 3 and 4.

5.

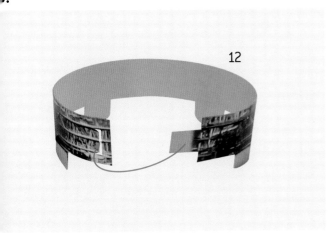

Insert the tab on piece 12 into the slot on piece 12.

6.

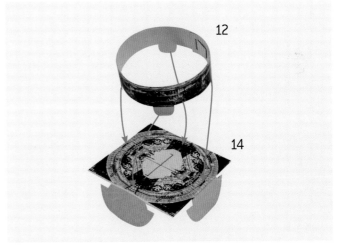

Insert piece 12 into the outer slots on piece 14. It doesn't matter which tabs go into which slots.

7.

Insert piece 15 into piece 14.
Slide piece 11 onto piece 15 and then into piece 14.

8.

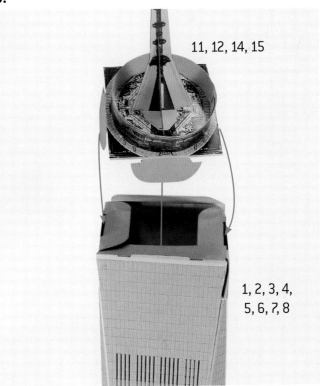

Insert piece 14 into the combined piece made up of pieces 1, 2, 3, 4, 5, 6, 7, and 8. It doesn't matter which tabs go into which slots.

9.

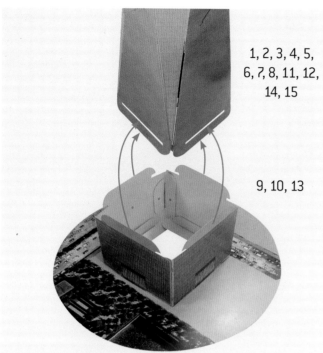

1, 2, 3, 4, 5,
6, 7, 8, 11, 12,
14, 15

9, 10, 13

Insert the 4 tabs in the top half of the model into the 4 slots on the bottom half. It doesn't matter which tabs go into which slots.

How to Build the Models

Only press out the pieces from the pages as you need them. This is because some pieces are numbered on the page rather than on the piece itself. Also, some pieces have artwork on both sides and you will sometimes need to know which side is the back.

Make all the folds on each piece once you have pressed it out, before following the step-by-step instructions. You will know where the folds need to be made as they are scored on the pieces.

Most of the folds in this book need to be made towards the back of the piece. Any folds that go in the opposite direction will be marked on the back of the piece with a red line along the length of the fold.

Fold Direction

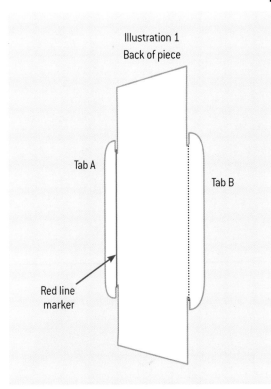

Illustration 1
Back of piece

Tab A

Tab B

Red line
marker

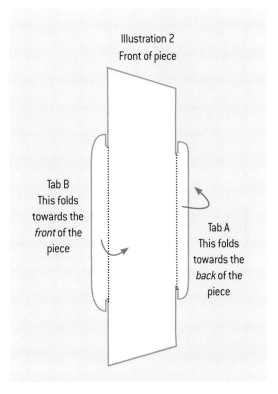

Illustration 2
Front of piece

Tab B
This folds
towards the
front of the
piece

Tab A
This folds
towards the
back of the
piece

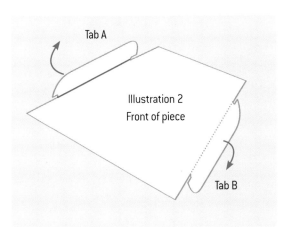

Tab A

Illustration 2
Front of piece

Tab B

With some of the smaller, fiddly tabs it can be helpful to use a pair of tweezers to pull the tabs through the slots.